A World of Drums

Julie Nickerson

A World of Drums

Text: Julie Nickerson
Publishers: Tania Mazzeo and Eliza Webb
Series consultant: Amanda Sutera
  Hands on Heads Consulting
Editor: Laken Ballinger
Project editor: Annabel Smith
Designer: Leigh Ashforth
Project designer: Danielle Maccarone
Permissions researcher: Liz McShane
Production controller: Renee Tome

Acknowledgements
We would like to thank the following for permission to reproduce
copyright material:

Front cover, p. 23 (bottom): iStock.com/S_Tanongsak; pp. 1, 23 (top right):
Shutterstock.com/sunabesyou; pp. 3, 12 (left), back cover (right):
Shutterstock.com/redstone; p. 4: Alamy Stock Photo/Danita Delimont; p. 5
(top): Shutterstock.com/ThomasLENNE, (bottom left): Shutterstock.
com/Sergej Cash, (bottom right): Shutterstock.com/Natalya Erofeeva; p. 6:
iStock.com/pepifoto; p. 7 (top): iStock.com/trekandshoot, (bottom): Aarthi
Rajesh Kumar; p. 8: Alamy Stock Photo/Galaxiid; p. 9: Alamy Stock
Photo/LMA/AW; p. 10: Shutterstock.com/yoshi0511; p. 11: Shutterstock.
com/mark stephens photography; p. 12 (right): iStock.com/track5; p. 13:
iStock.com/Sandra Milena Valero Orjuela; p. 14: Pixabay/allybally4b; p. 15:
iStock.com/TwilightShow; p. 16: Getty Images/Gijsbert Hanekroot; p. 17:
Getty Images/The Washington Post; p. 18: Alamy Stock Photo/WENN
Rights Ltd; p. 19: Getty Images/Jack Vartoogian; p. 21: iStock.com/DjelicS;
p. 22: Alamy Stock Photo/DC Newsfeed; p. 23 (top left): Getty Images/Rob
Lewine; pp. 23 (top middle), 24: Shutterstock.com/StockImageFactory.
com; back cover (left): Shutterstock.com/In Green

Every effort has been made to trace and acknowledge copyright.
However, if any infringement has occurred, the publishers tender their
apologies and invite the copyright holders to contact them.

NovaStar

Text © 2024 Cengage Learning Australia Pty Limited

ISBN 978 0 17 033390 0

Cengage Learning Australia
Level 5, 80 Dorcas Street
Southbank VIC 3006 Australia
Phone: 1300 790 853
Email: aust.nelsonprimary@cengage.com

For learning solutions, visit **cengage.com.au**

Printed in China by 1010 Printing International Ltd
1 2 3 4 5 6 7 28 27 26 25 24

*Nelson acknowledges the Traditional Owners and Custodians
of the lands of all First Nations Peoples. We pay respect
to Elders past and present, and extend that respect to
all First Nations Peoples today.*

Contents

Here Come the Drums!

Bang! Boom! Can you hear the drums? Drums are **percussion instruments**. These are instruments that you hit or shake to make a sound. Drums can make a steady **beat** for a song or a piece of music.

Girls in Cambodia, Asia, play drums and sing to the beat.

Most drums are round and have two parts. The body, or shell, of a drum is a hollow **cylinder**, often made of wood. Stretched tightly over the body is the drum's head. This is the part that you hit. Most modern drum heads are made of strong plastic.

The body of this drum is made of wood and is hollow on the inside.

Sticks or Hands

Drums can be hit with your hands or with drumsticks. Hitting a drum with your hands or with drumsticks makes a different sound.

Drum kits are made up of several drums and **cymbals**. A drum kit has a bass (say: *base*) drum, a snare drum and tom-toms. Each part of a drum kit makes a different sound.

The tom-toms make high and low sounds based on their different sizes.

The snare drum makes a loud, sharp sound.

The cymbals make a high, crashing sound.

The bass drum makes a deep, low sound.

Electronic drum kits are popular with drummers of all ages. An electronic drum kit allows you to make the sounds of lots of different drums. You can change the sounds by simply pushing a button. You can then hear the drums through headphones or speakers.

Electronic drum kits usually have smaller drums and cymbals than a regular drum kit.

The Fastest Drumming

In 2021, an 11-year-old boy from Australia named Pritish A R broke the world record for the fastest drumming with drumsticks. He was able to hit his drum almost 2400 times in one minute. That's nearly 40 times every second!

Drums
from Around the World

Different kinds of drums are played all over the world. They come in many shapes and sizes.

Drums are different all around the world, such as these ones made in the Pacific Islands.

Warup

The *warup*, or *buruburu*, is a wooden drum from the Torres Strait Islands, Australia. This drum is very important to Torres Strait Islander peoples. It is used in celebrations and to tell stories with song and dance. The drum can be decorated with shells, nuts, feathers or carvings of animals. The shells and nuts rattle when the drum is hit.

This warup is decorated with feathers and shells.

The drum head of the warup is made from the skin of a large lizard or snake. Feathers from birds called cassowaries are often used as decorations. These dark feathers look like hair.

Taiko

Japanese drums are called *taiko*. There are many kinds of taiko, and they all make different sounds. Taiko have been around for about 1500 years and are still used in festivals, plays and **ceremonies**. Groups of taiko players often perform at **multicultural** festivals around the world. The music they play is loud, fast and fun!

Taiko can be placed on stands so that it's easy for the drummers to play them.

A group of drummers play taiko during a performance in Japan.

Djembe

The *djembe* (say: *jem-bay*) from West Africa is played by slapping the drum head with hands or fingers. Although you only use your hands to play it, this drum can make loud noises and many different sounds.

Djembe are painted in lots of different colours and patterns.

Djembe are often played at traditional ceremonies, and even at weddings. Some djembe drums are quite colourful!

A djembe is played at an African concert.

CheonGo Drum

The world's largest drum is the *CheonGo* drum in South Korea. This enormous drum is 6 metres tall and just over 5 metres wide. Can you guess how heavy it is? It weighs 7 **tonnes** – the same as a large elephant! The giant drumstick is so heavy, you need two hands to lift it.

The CheonGo drum is a traditional Korean drum. It is beautifully decorated with colourful patterns.

A man hits the huge CheonGo drum in South Korea.

The CheonGo drum looks similar to this traditional Korean drum at a palace in South Korea – but much bigger!

Famous Drummers

Some drummers are famous for their speed, amazing skills and exciting playing.

Dave Grohl

Dave Grohl was the drummer for the US rock group Nirvana, which became famous in the early 1990s. But Dave never took any drumming lessons. Instead, he learned to play by hitting pillows while listening to his favourite drummers.
He watched and listened to drummers such as John Bonham from the English rock group Led Zeppelin, one of the world's fastest and most powerful drummers. Dave later started the rock group Foo Fighters.

John Bonham
of Led Zeppelin

Dave Grohl plays drums at a performance in the USA.

Travis Barker

Travis Barker is a US drummer for the rock group Blink-182. He has been playing the drums since he was only four years old. He is famous for his drumming skills in different kinds of music, such as rock, hip-hop and rap.

Travis Barker plays drums with Blink–182.

Cindy Blackman

Cindy Blackman is a drummer from the USA who played for singer Lenny Kravitz for 18 years. She is known for her powerful drumming **style**, and she enjoys playing both jazz and rock music.

Cindy Blackman plays at a jazz festival in the USA.

How to Find the Beat

Drummers need to find the beat of the music.
You can practise this, too, even if you don't own a drum.

Steps

1. Put on some music that you enjoy.

2. Sit quietly and listen for the beat. The beat sounds like the heartbeat of the music.

3. Tap the beat on your right knee with your right hand.

4. Change hands, and tap the beat on your left knee.

5. Practise lifting your arms higher in between tapping your knees to make the sound louder. Then, use both hands to tap both knees.

6. Try to move your arms faster or slower and still keep in time with the music.

7. Have fun, and pretend you're playing the drums!

Listen for the beat of the music and have fun!

21

Keep Playing the Drums!

Drums are popular instruments and have many uses. You might see them at a concert or at a festival. People of all ages from all over the world can play the drums.

A drum group performs at a street band festival in Scotland.

Drummers play along with the beat of the music.
If you have a chance to listen to or play the drums,
you are sure to enjoy yourself!

Glossary

beat (*noun*)	a steady count heard or felt in music
ceremonies (*noun*)	traditional events to celebrate something special
cylinder (*noun*)	a long rounded shape with flat ends, like a pole
cymbals (*noun*)	musical instruments shaped like round metal plates
electronic (*adjective*)	using electricity to work
multicultural (*adjective*)	from many different countries or places
percussion instruments (*noun*)	instruments played by hitting them
style (*noun*)	the way something is done
tonnes (*noun*)	weights equal to 1000 kilograms

Index

NovaStar

Comprehension ★ Knowledge ★ Engagement

If you enjoyed this book, try these!

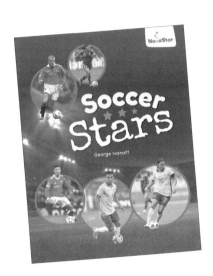

Looking for more titles in this series?

Go to nelsonprimary.com.au/novastar

Drums are instruments that are played by
people all over the world. They come in many
shapes and make lots of different sounds.
Learning to find the beat like a drummer is a fun way
to enjoy some of your favourite music!

Comprehension ★ Knowledge ★ Engagement

ISBN 978-0170333900

9 780170 333900